GW00419886

B. McRobert

HUMANS AS PETS

written and illustrated by

DAVID WESTWOOD

TWO HEADS PUBLISHING

WELCOME
TO THE
WONDERFUL
WORLD OF
CATS...

SMUDGE

Thanks to
John Berley, Robert Bloomfield, Janet Bonthron,
Sharon Dirnberger, Marilyn Fleming, Charles Frewin, Rudy Garza,
Susan Kelly, Kathy Toguchi and the resources of the vast
Toguchi Cat Library, Mike Rossi, and of course little Schmickels.

Training your Hosts, part 1

Cats, no less liquid than their shadows,
offer no angles to the wind.
They slip, diminished, neat, through loopholes
less than themselves.
— A S J Tessimond, *Cats*

Servants, waking up the

Humans are lazy and will stay in bed long past five a.m. if allowed, believe it or not. Especially on Saturdays and Sundays, when for some perverse reason they become worse.

In order to be served breakfast when you wish, you must learn to wake them, and this can be accomplished in a variety of ways. Some felines use the traditional face-lick, but if this isn't your style try *treading* on the face, an unsubtle but always effective solution.

Others are walking along the dressing table and knocking things off with a satisfying smash, howling near their ears, or climbing under the sheets and biting toes, disgusting though the latter may seem.

Modern tricks also include tampering with their electronic gadgets. Stepping on the buttons of an answering machine, working computer keyboard or fax can yield instant response, as will knocking a phone off its hook to elicit its annoying beep.

THE CURL

Naps, the importance of

We, on the other paw, are never lazy. We sleep at many times of the day, it's true, but this is because our evolutionary *raison d'etre* has for the most part been removed, now that our prey comes pre-killed in Whiskas cans. As a consequence our alertness is required less, and we are able to both conserve our resources and remain decorative, a uniquely feline feat.

We possess the true knack of taking our ease

THE STRETCH

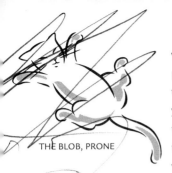

THE BLOB, PRONE

when and where we please. You must learn to ignore requests from your humans to do things when they want to, just because it fits within *their* active cycle.

If you let them, they'll expect you to eat when they do, go out when they do, even stare at that picture-box thing when they do. Lost to them are the joys of capering around in the middle of the night, the ecstasies of conking out at nine, eleven, one, three, five, and any and all hours of the day.

Eventually you should be able to disrupt their schedules to a point where they lose all confidence in the solidity of their routine, and anything you want to do will be acceptable at any time.

Whatever you do, don't adapt to theirs. You need your sixteen hours.

THE BLOB, SUPINE

Meals, contents of

Twolegs tend to serve the cheapest trash possible, unless you let them know in no uncertain terms that this is unacceptable cuisine for your discriminating palate. They're descended from *apes*, remember, so don't expect any gustatory sophistication from creatures who evolved on bananas and nuts. They can't comprehend the importance of the requisite *rankness* of meat, the proper *gameyness* of poultry, the...well, the *fishyness* of fish.

Some misguided individuals even try to turn us into *vegetarians*, of all things, which is not only naïve but dangerous, since we're dyed-in-the-wool, card-carrying carnivores. Perhaps they'd like to fill their car's petrol tank with water and see how well it runs.

If you're in any doubt about what's put in front of you, turn up your nose with disdain and refuse to eat. It's worth the few hours of hunger — the guilt and worry that you'll be putting your servants through makes them more malleable. Eventually, in a panic that you might wither away and die on them (yeah, right), they'll parade before you every possible delicacy until you relent and accept one. How about the *Pilchards in Prawn Jelly* today? Or *Mackerel in Aspic*? No, perhaps the *Rabbit and Duck*...though that *Turkey and Liver* does sound tempting, doesn't it? Then again, *Salmon and Tuna* might be tasty...

Take your time, and even when they have managed to suit your taste, don't forget to keep them on their toes by occasionally sending it back.

If worst comes to worst and your serfs *still* try to feed you substandard meals, try those nice people next door.

Granted, being taken for

Humans are understandably proud of our species' unique grace and beauty but tend to lapse into thinking of us, if permitted, as docile and ornamental, instead of the savage hunters we are. This complacency requires shattering once in a while, and you can use your inventiveness to find

ways that are fun and interesting. A tried and tested trick is biting the hand that feeds you. Simply act playful and silly, then when the staffmember you wish to teach a lesson has its guard down, give its hand a bite or swipe nasty enough to draw blood.

Abandonment, dealing with

It's customary to ignore humans on their return, making them work for your reluctant acceptance and affection. Don't overdo the affection bit, either. The less you give the more they'll want to serve, in the desperate hope that you may condescend to sit on their lap and purr for a while. By all means do so, but as soon as they're relaxed, dig in the claws and leap away.

Medium-length absences, often obscurely referred to as 'dirty weekends' or 'popping in' on someone, require medium-strength reprisals. Tripping up servants by walking between their legs is easy and effective.

Long absences, called 'holidays,' constitute crimes that call for stiffer punishment, even if your servants have subcontracted to another to 'look in on you' and make sure your dish is full. Make as much mess as a manic feline can, letting them know that if they want  the place to stay *intact*, they'd better stay *inside*.

Hair, transferring the gift of

Twolegs are in awe of our silky fur, being mostly bald themselves. This is why they resort to covering themselves with those awful pieces of fabric and, God forbid, animal skins.

In a concession to their embarrassingly naked state, we have a duty to share our wealth. Whenever possible, liberally deposit tufts of your hair on articles of their treasured clothing, choosing a colour that contrasts with that of your coat so they'll be sure to notice and be suitably grateful. Leaving hair on furniture is appropriate too, as well

as rugs, towels, bed-
spreads and food.

You Persians
should have no prob-
lem with this, whereas
you shorthairs will
have to work a little
harder. If for some

reason your fur stays put, then try to periodically
cough up a good, compact furball for them to
keep as a souvenir.

Intimidation, tactics for

Your staff long ago gave up their individuality,
like dogs, budgerigars and goldfish, in exchange for
safety and shelter. Because of this they can forget
that we are the lords of creation, and assume that
cats, too, are equally subservient to the same rules
and confinements they've chosen to live within.
(We, needless to say, are subservient to nothing at
all.) So in order to maintain your station and
retain their respect, you'll need to put a good scare
up them every now and then.

Staring spookily at humans for an inordinately

long time makes them exquisitely uncomfortable, and a sudden insane lunge for no apparent reason is always good to get the adrenaline flowing though their sluggish bodies. Our favourite is the ol' arching the back and hissing at something invisible routine. This latter brings out their latent primate fears of ghosts and can be kept up indefinitely (though not *too* often).

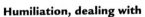

Humiliation, dealing with

It's not often we cats find ourselves in embarrassing situations, since we're normally so poised and coordinated. But sometimes something happens, like being caught in mid-pooh by a stranger. It's bad enough being seen by *anyone* at such a time, since in the wild we would always wait for total privacy, but the *cleaner*? How gauche.

Often we're taken completely by surprise by

the sudden appearance of The Hoover Monster. Then there's those absurd Elizabethan collars the servants make us wear when we've been biting at fleas or mites so much that our fur is suffering.

Occasionally we might miss something we were jumping for, or the damn thing will be on castors and skid when we reach it, dumping us unceremoniously on the floor. Then there's getting our head stuck in a jar while investigating, and the worst of all, falling in the toilet bowl while drinking. And these are often compounded by human laughter if caught red-pawed.

Well, inept though we might appear for a second, *never* admit it. Use your loudest *ffft* snort, lash your tail from side to side in anger, and either hide for a while or scratch something to show you haven't lost your touch. Don't come when called, and use all your irritation techniques to make your menials pay.

Transport

Of course, we don't *really* mind being in the cat carrier — we just pretend to hate it. In reality, we love to be carried instead of having to walk somewhere. It's just the kind of *places* we're taken to in the thing — like the vet, to have things cut off, sewn up, or injected (not to mention enduring the rectal thermometer) — that we have a beef (or perhaps a tuna) about.

In view of these dubious destinations, hide the moment the carrier is brought out, and make your Bigs work hard to cajole you into entering. Yowl pathetically during the journey, and if in a car or public transportation feel free to urinate at will.

Family, additions to yours

You queens can bring much joy into the paltry, boring lives of your menials by favouring them with an spectacular litter of your own. Surprise is

the key here, so apart from sneaking out for your sexual assignations without their knowledge, try to mate with as many toms as possible, giving your brood that rainbow spread of colour variation that they love so much. And the wonderful thing is, you'll be capable of producing a hundred or more kittens in your lifetime.

Toms: though you may be without a female in your house, you can still, of course, participate in the kitten manufacturing process in the traditional ways. Don't be shy in showing your maleness around the home with your piercing calls and the frequent squirting of your particular carnal cologne. (If not allowed out you may resort to trouser-humping, even though it's more commonly a gesture associated with dogs.) And returning home torn and bloody after those exhilarating territorial fights with the other neighbourhood males is always effective in eliciting the ministrations of mercy that make humans so useful.

Family, additions to theirs

Once in a while your domestic help will find the need to reproduce. This is irritating and the results are invariably hideous, but remember that this is where new maids and butlers come from. Besides, they don't do it very often and don't produce big litters.

But they do tend to fawn over the new arrival for an irresponsibly long time, and will temporarily forget your needs if you don't remind them who's in charge. Use the intimidation tactics discussed above, plus ignoring and surliness. Bear in mind that you can add a piquant sense of danger to any action by performing it near the newborn human, which will make its parents take instant notice of you.

Eventually they'll relearn to appreciate your fastidious cleanliness, qualities only manifested by their babies after twenty years or so, if at all. But the complexities of having children around deserves its own section:

Human children, dealing with

All infants need coaching by the mother in

learning their way around, feline no less than human. The only trouble is, *ours* are finished in a couple of months, whereas with simian babies it seems their drooling, puking infancy is endless.

When your servants litter, you'll be stuck with this nasty, smelly, noisy lump for — brace yourself — most of your life. Makes you wish a short trip to the vet could've neutered them too, doesn't it? Yes, resign yourself to the crying, the crawling, and when they're old enough to be ambulatory the most annoying of all: *grabbing and poking at Kitty.*

1...2....3....4...

Little boys are worst in this, and if you're wise you'll avoid them at all times. Until they're eighteen or so, anyway, by which time they'll hopefully have left to torment someone else.

These painful experiments must be endured *without triggering your normal defensive response,*

though. Gashing their offspring will make your servants upset enough to give you to someone else
(who could be worse), or have you 'put down.'
Now none of us knows exactly *where* we're put
when we're put down (some cats think Australia*),
but it must be worse** or it wouldn't be threat-
ened as a punishment. Wherever it might be, best
not to find out.

*The fact that Australia is the only inhabited continent sadly lacking
in indigenous felines lends credence to this theory. **Definitely Australia.*

Other animals, enduring the presence of

In some situations we are expected to cohabit
with members of species other than human, name-
ly *dogs* but sometimes anything from gerbils to
ducks. These intrusions on our turf can be borne,
provided these lower orders are taught their place.

It's not necessary to terrorise them for ever,
but a little at first establishes the proper pecking
order. Brutality is not required; unpredictability is
the key, keeping them off-balance and defensive.
Thereafter, the occasional hiss should be sufficient
to keep them in line.

Given a little time to adjust, we can live successfully with other animals, though their relative underdevelopment and severely limited social skills can be numbingly boring.

Display, self-

Acknowledging our refinement and elegant splendour, humans have shrewdly provided openings in our houses for us to display ourselves to the rest of the world. These transparent openings, called *windows*, serve both as podiums for our preening and, when weather permits, a sun bath. It is thus another duty of ours to use these windows as a kind of gallery in which to exhibit the status of our domestics.

Strangely, even cat-less houses sport windows, which goes to show that cat display has entered human architecture as a classic, symbolic feature, like columns and arches.

Cattish/English Dictionary

Cats seem to go on the principle that
it never does any harm to ask for what you want.
— *Joseph Wood Krutch*

*Some sounds in Cattish have different meanings,
depending on inflection, context and volume.*

meow?

Food? Stroke? Can I have some? Aren't you
awake yet? Huh? Were you speaking to me?

meow

Notice me. Move. Feed me. More.

MEOW!

Watch out — here I come! Hey, you! No! Yes!
Not the rap album again!

prr

Nice.

prrrr

Very nice.

prrrrrrrrrrrrrrrr

Ahhhhhhh. I wonder what the poor people are doing.

rrrrrRRRRROWWWWWW!

This is my garden/dustbin/dead bird/female.

rrrRRROWWwww

Well don't let it happen again.

RRREEEOW!

You sat/trod on me, idiot.

weeeeeowww

Let me out. Let me in. Let me out again.

WEEeeoooOWWWEeeoooowwWWWWW

Come, my love, and let us join in temporary matrimony.

fft

Ugh. Nasty. Gross.

fffft

No, I don't think so.

fffffffffffft!

Get that out of my face!

sssssssssssst!

One step nearer and I'll rip your nose off.

yawn

Oh, *pleeease*. Wake me when there's something *interesting* going on.

Cat Graffiti

Fluffy has distemper

Black Panthers

Ginger has sardine breath

Kitty was here

Lions rule

Marmalade likes ~~dashunts~~ ~~daschhunds~~ sausage dogs

Eat Grass and puke

Reasons why Humans

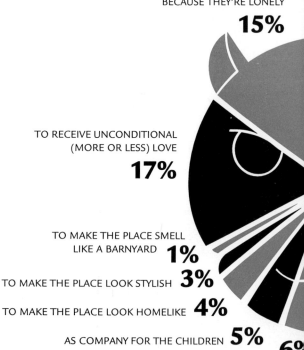

BECAUSE THEY'RE LONELY
15%

TO RECEIVE UNCONDITIONAL
(MORE OR LESS) LOVE
17%

TO MAKE THE PLACE SMELL
LIKE A BARNYARD **1%**

TO MAKE THE PLACE LOOK STYLISH **3%**

TO MAKE THE PLACE LOOK HOMELIKE **4%**

AS COMPANY FOR THE CHILDREN **5%**

6%

TO HAVE SOMEONE TO SER`

keep Cats

TO HAVE A SIMPLE RELATIONSHIP (FOR A CHANGE)
WITH SOMETHING THAT DOESN'T TALK BACK (MUCH)

13%

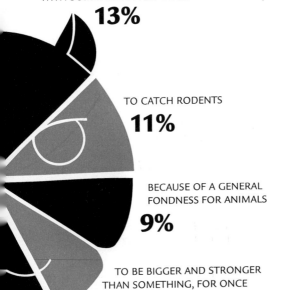

TO CATCH RODENTS
11%

BECAUSE OF A GENERAL
FONDNESS FOR ANIMALS

9%

TO BE BIGGER AND STRONGER
THAN SOMETHING, FOR ONCE

8%

BECAUSE WE'RE CHEAPER THAN A KID,
DON'T LIVE AS LONG, AND DON'T HAVE TO BE
CLOTHED AND PUT THROUGH SCHOOL **7%**

How Humans see you

How you really are

Types of Cat 'Owner'

> ...This is the cat
> That killed the rat
> That ate the malt
> That lay in the house that Jack built.
> — *Nurse Truelove's New Year's Gift, 1755*

Families

This is by far the most common situation in which a self-respecting cat can find him- or herself. Dealing with small children, as described above, can be traumatic, but this is on the whole a gratifying nest type since there's always attention to be had from someone. At least one of the family is generally a soft touch and can be manipulated relentlessly. In fact, for cats with large appetites it's often possible to elicit meals from more than one human, using stealth and cunning.

29

Families also tend to possess a garden that you can claim as your own, stalking suburban songbirds and small pets that next-door neighbours mistakenly let loose for walkies.

Pensioners

These are often disproportionately women, since the human female seems to kill off the male after a while and live alone. Perhaps she eats him, we're not sure. But anyway, we are supremely important to them, since they stay in the nest a lot and need our affectionate company.

Hold down the tripping and zooming with these types — they're frail and may not recover from any sudden surprises. Though predictable, they can be touchingly loving and while they tire easily, they still enjoy serving. Besides, they always have balls of yarn to attack. And you can always sneak out occasionally for a bit of fun.

Career couples

Lately more and more couples are choosing to stay childless and just work a lot. In the good old days there was either one at home most of the time, or at least not too much of the day spent away by both. But this new system means you'll have the nest to yourself an uncomfortable amount.

You can try the trashing techniques covered earlier, but this obsessive need to work is displacement behaviour that stems from their not having a little servant or two to focus their energies, and as a consequence it goes deep and is difficult to undo.

If possible, supply them with a batch or two of yours, which may make them more homebound. But chances are your reproductive capabilities have been tampered with. If so, you may have to make your loneliness known by pitiful mewing, forlorn gazing from the window as they leave, and hanging out with any stuffed animal you can find. With any luck this will result in their bringing in another cat as a companion.

Single men

Some men are quite adequate domestics, as nurturing as any female, family or senior. Others, however, are frustrated dog persons — you can tell: they're embarrassed at living with a cat because they don't consider it macho enough. Some part of them really wants a Rottweiler or Pit Bull, and they probably either inherited you from an old girlfriend or a mum that took the dirt nap, or just thought you'd be less trouble. It's up to you to make this kind of human's life miserable, in the hope that you'll be transferred to a home with a more amenable servant.

But save your worst behaviour for those times he's trying to get intimate with his lover. When he

puts his face on hers, leap on them hissing and spitting, scratching her clothing. This should shatter the romantic ambience sufficiently, but if more is needed go berserk in the bedroom. Use your 'baby being tortured' voice and fling yourself around the walls like a demented bat.

The human male will be mortified, the female will reject him as a prospective partner, and he should either a) treat you better, or b) give you to someone who will. Of course, there's always c) get violent, in which case you'll have to find a new nest as quickly as felinely possible.

Farmers

A rural domain can provide a most beneficial life for a feline, as long as you like catching your food on the hoof, as it were, as will probably be expected of you.

Your territory will be large, there'll be lots of big, dumb animals to spook and annoy, and rodents by the barnful. Of course, if you're one of those urbane, effete 'I only eat out of tins' types this will be quite an adjustment, but a worthwhile one. (Food that wriggles is so much more fun.)

This is, after all, closer to our ancestral habitat than some one-bedroom cubicle in a building that should've been condemned five  monarchies ago. Then again, a few scruffy fields of rapeseed and rhubarb is not exactly the foothills of Kilimanjaro either, but at least it's a kind of freedom not found in the city.

Drawbacks are burrs in the fur, ticks in the ears and becoming a kind of flea bus, but what are humans for if not for grooming? Those opposable thumbs are useful for something, after all.

This is also a situation in which we come up against creatures with almost equally powerful predator skills, and who can catch us off-guard if we're not careful. Foxes, large psychotic and/or very hungry dogs, and in some countries coyotes, wolves, wolverines, hyenas and skunks should be steered well clear of. We may be smarter, but they don't care that we're more edified, only that we're edible.

Teens

Living with teenage or twentysomething Bigs is usually a serious mistake, since at those ages they're throwbacks to the barbarian. They'll forget to feed you, change the litterbox, or put down fresh water. In fact, they'll often forget to come home for days, and when they finally do you'll wish they hadn't. They'll bring over all kinds of lowlife friends, have loud parties until all hours and play noises of indescribable abrasiveness.

If you find yourself in this kind of predicament your best bets are twofold. One, the obvious, is to move. The second is to manage to dye yourself an unnatural colour and, if possible, trim or singe one side of your fur radically. By this method you'll brand yourself cool, or at least odd, and they'll include you in their circle of friends instead of thinking of you as just some domestic obligation.

Squatters, Hell's Angels, etc

Sadly, these kind of humans embody the worst traits of teens, small boys and single men combined. If this suits your temperament, fine, but many of us dislike drinking rainwater out of rusty hubcaps, defecating in an old tyre and dumpster-dining on things like cheese and onion crisps and fish skins.

Better to try and find an old lady on one of her trips to and from the shops and latch on, in the hope that she'll take you home.

Stray/Homeless

Not many of us choose the homeless life, but end up vagrant by default. And like other indigent creatures, once outside the pale of civilisation it's very difficult to reenter. Cats are a little better off than most in that we can still keep ourselves clean, and therein lies our salvation.

For those who pine after the soft suburban lifestyle, find an area you'd like to live in, isolate a houseful of humans you think could serve your purposes, preen carefully and adopt them with your winning, kittenish ways.

Play hard to get at first, so as not to seem too eager, then condescend to accept the occasional saucer of water. Then just hang around more and more until the children make a fuss if you leave. By that time you've won, and you can move in.

Laboratory scientists

Never, ever, go along with any humans wearing white coats or who smell of anæsthetic, no matter how tasty their treats. Each year, mogs by the million disappear into so-called 'scientific establishments' and are never seen again. Rumours abound as to what actually happens inside, but whatever it is you don't want it to happen to you.

If you've had the misfortune to be born in one of these places, or taken when you were a kitten and too small to know what was going on, escape at all costs. If you can't get out of the cage, enlist the help of one of the chimps. They're related to humans and can work out the locks.

Humans vs Felines

Cats and monkeys, monkeys and cats —
all human life is there.
— *Henry James*

HUMANS	**CATS**
Need to wear clothes.	Grow our own, thanks.
Need to join athletic clubs.	The whole house is our gym.
Need to work for a living.	Zzzzzzzzzzzzzzzz.
Need to pay taxes, rates, insurance premiums, rent/ mortgage payments, car instalments, etc.	Hahaha.

HUMANS	**CATS**
Need long preambles to sex.	Just get on with it.
Need to rear offspring for years.	Hey — it's been three months. There's the door.
Need to sleep in beds.	But *everything's* a bed, isn't it?
Need to use cosmetics.	Always look good.
Need to wash with water.	Self-cleaning.
Need to cook.	Are fed.
Need to think.	Huh?

Key elements of Humans

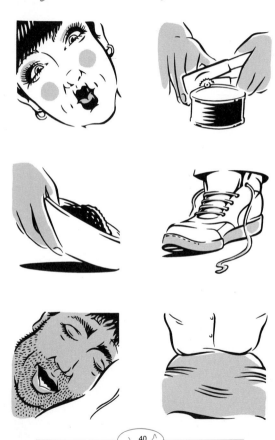

English/Cattish Dictionary

If a man could be crossed with a cat,
it would improve man but deteriorate the cat.
— *Mark Twain*

Though they tend to make a lot of them, few noises
humans make have much relevance,
except for the following:

Breakfast!

Time to eat.

Lunch!

Time to eat.

Dinner!

Time to eat.

Mouse!

Time to hunt, then eat.

Kitty?

Time to ignore.

Here, KittyKittyKitty!

Time to hide.

Mumble mumble Vet mumble mumble

Time to split.

Oooooh darling! Yes! Yes!

Time to investigate.

No!

OK, go ahead.

Stop that!

That's nice, carry on.

Bad cat!

Good cat.

Training your Hosts, part II

For I will consider my cat Jeoffry.
For he is the servant of the Living God,
duly and daily serving Him.
— *Christopher Smart, Jubilate Agno*

Chairs, the claiming of

One of the many peculiarities of twolegs is the belief that chairs, sofas and stools are provided for their benefit. This typifies the pathetically limited understanding of their kind for the Great Hierarchy of Life, of which we are of course the zenith. While it's true that having only two legs and a remarkably clunky and inflexible skeleton means they must rest

in specially-shaped receptacles (instead of, like *felidæ*, anywhere we damn well please), always remember that *nothing* in the home is theirs.

If you ever suspect some benighted human

seems to be thinking proprietorially about a particular chair, claim it for a few days at a stretch. Scratch and hiss demoniacally if it attempts to sit on the chair while you're in residence, and you'll find in a few days they'll have forgotten they ever considered it their own. Or at least be too frightened to try it again.

Toyness

A key fact sadly lost by some of us on leaving the innocent bliss of kittenhood is that *everything is a toy*. The most inanimate objects can be animated if you've retained the knack, from polystyrene packing peanuts to those flimsy undergarments in the bedroom (do humans actually wear this stuff?). Matchbooks, pencils, plants, cosmetics, condoms, credit cards, ping pong balls, false teeth — the list is endless. That alarm clock — isn't it a giant silhouette of...a *mouse*? That glass thing — it's

not a knickknack, it's a *cockroach*! Those shoelaces — *worms*! *Snakes*! Pounce! Kill! Eat!

And as for other creatures, they can be even more satisfying to fool around with. Who can forget the spectacular reaction of a caged bird when we stick our nose between the bars and display our teeth?* How delicious to bait a dog and then suddenly slash mercilessly at its fat, glossy nose. And members of *Homo sapiens*, of course, are endless fun to harass and confuse. They even recognise our play needs to such an extent that they order a bundle of fresh toy, called a *newspaper*, to be delivered for us every morning.

Never give up the playfulness that makes we cats such a joy to be around. Be creative. Suspend that boring belief in reality long enough to imbue anything with life and swat at it, drag it around, pounce on it and rip it to shreds.

Then, naturally, play with the shreds.

*Stay away from the parrot.

Affection, displays of

One of the many misunderstandings of our behaviour is the human interpretation of what appears to them to be feline *affection*. We are truly loving, as duly noted under *Love, being the source of*, but sometimes other actions can be mistakenly assumed to be affectionate. What looks to them like a fond snuggle by their four-legged friend is, of course, your *allomarking* — using the mouth, then forehead, cheek and entire length of your body to transfer scent from glands in your head and tail to your servant, now marked as your property.

Another misunderstood action is licking. Instead of being an expression of love or devotion, we're just using our raspy tongue in racially-remembered instincts. Primarily the cleaning reflex — we are such fastidious creatures, after all. Bigs have lost the ability to lick themselves clean, though you can sometimes catch them licking each other. Vestigial grooming behaviour, presumably.

Scratching, the necessity of

A related issue is scratching, the overwhelming need to tatter something with our claws. Vets try to tell our staff that scratching is not to *sharpen* claws but to dull and trim them, to remove old claw sheaths and reveal the new.

But as we know, scratching is another kind of territorial mark, as equally fulfilling to deliver as the spray. Who of us hasn't experienced the thrill of developing one's own style of ripping ritzy fabric from the arm of the loveseat? What cat can deny itself the gouging of expensive wallpaper, costly cushions? What feline can decline the deep and damaging tear of nylons, lace curtains, silk dresses and shirts, the satisfying shred of a sock?

Try not to get carried away on some crazed scratch-a-thon though, or the cruel bipeds will

have your claws hacked out, and then you won't be able to climb or protect yourself on the street. It makes you wonder — if they don't want us to scratch they remove our claws; if they don't want us to mate they take away our equipment. What if we eat too much? Will they have our tongues cut out? The Manx must've *really* pissed them off.

Just be thankful that those 'cat's eyes' in the road are really just glass, and that catgut comes from sheep.

Zoomies, the need for

Humans often assume, because of our supreme ability to relax and relish the sensuousness of our surroundings, that we are slothful and indolent. Consequently it often becomes necessary to mount a display of your athletic powers just to put them in their place.

All this requires is to suddenly dash madly from room to room, bookcase to ottoman, sink to sofa. Climb the Christmas tree, whack the blinds, chase toilet articles around the bathtub. In the middle of the night. And don't overlook the curtains in that Olympic spring for the ceiling. Not all the time, of course — no need to burn off too much energy unnecessarily — but more as a kind of punctuation to your usual languid existence.

Everyone knows a cheetah can reach 100km/h during a chase, but did you know *Felis catus*, on hearing the can opener, has been clocked at 120 in that mad dash between bedroom and kitchen?

Zooming

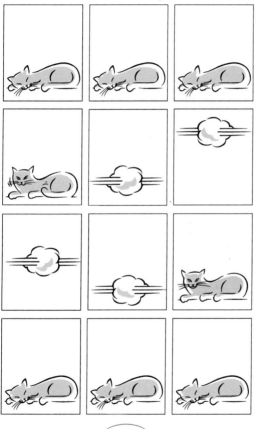

But don't try this in the street. Humans, lethargic lumps that they are, drive everywhere in metal boxes they can barely control, have reflexes slower than those of a hippo, and *they* can't see in the dark.

Litter box, use of

It's quaint, but your hosts will expect you to relieve yourself in a tray full of perfumed aqua gravel parked conspicuously in the traffic flow of the house. This can be, needless to say, humiliating. To the descendants of Raj, whose muscular, tawny presence claimed the entire prairie as her pissoir, this is the ultimate in insult.

Humans also like to ignore the state of the litterbox until *their* senses are reminded it needs cleaning. But as every animal knows,  their noses have degenerated to the point of uselessness, so what smells a little to them has been reeking to us for weeks. The usual punishment meted out for this negligence is random defecation on your part, in intimate areas like the bedroom.

Territory, the marking of

Those giant bipeds who run your house have little concept of territory. They can claim only the few cramped rooms you all inhabit, and even then the real owner is some bank. (Sometimes their children will make a pathetic effort to tag their neighbourhoods with spray cans, but this is typically crude. And occasionally a male can be seen identifying an alley after a few drinks at his local, but this is random.) So it's not surprising that marking territory is outside their limited ken. Strangely, they tend to always urinate in the same place, which doesn't serve to tell their friends anything about who they are or what they've been up to, as does our informative little message.

As a result they entirely miss our need to constantly renew our scents on the boundaries of our turf. (Otherwise the neighbourhood would go, after all, to the dogs.) These olfactorily-challenged creatures can't comprehend that we may own the next four houses, half the street, a critical alley crossroad, and that these properties need *reclaiming* regularly. Nor do they grasp that a tom's territory is *ten times* larger than a female's, and takes consequently ten times more effort to police it. (Not to mention ten times more urine.)

No, let's face it, they'll never be successfully trained in this, and you'll have to resign yourself to their noncomprehension every time you go out, come in, go out, come in and want to go out again. Exasperating, but there it is.

Hiding, the art of

Having great height has its advantages, which is why we keep humans around for reaching things on the top shelves, but one of the problems with being a giant is that you can't indulge in *hiding*, one of our most rewarding skills. Their children, of course, revel in it for as long as they can, but soon they grow too massive to ever be lost by anyone. Unfortunately.

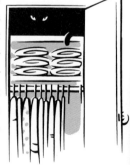

We, on the other hand, are masters of magic, able to disappear at will. This is a useful knack when your servants require you for something that doesn't interest you, or in order to scold them for bad food, bad music, bad manners or some other indiscretion. And because of our compactness and flexibility our choices are endless: beds, boxes, laundry baskets and bags, shelves and drawers, wardrobes, cupboards and closets, cars, cartons, pots and pans, roofs and gutters, chimneys and trees.

As a general rule, watch out for things with engines in them, things with dogs in them, things that are thrown out of windows, down chutes, mashed in big lorries or recycled. Also, try not to get too high in the trees, or you'll have to be rescued by men in funny hats from a big red ladder vehicle, and it's embarrassing.

Allergies, sufferers of

Some poor humans are handicapped with an inability to appreciate the feline race without sneezes, wheezes, watering eyes and a difficulty in breathing. This probably stems from some mutation or other genetic defect. You'll easily be able to recognise them: One day your servant will bring home a new lover and they'll cringe at the sight of you. All evening they'll try to keep as far away from you as they possibly can.

Don't worry. Offensive as is the mere presence of someone who can't treasure *us*, lords of the hearth that we are, these unfortunates can be easily dealt with. Once they're seated, jump in their lap, rub against them, scratch yourself with abandon and divest yourself of as much hair as you can muster. This will instantly ensure you'll never have to traffic with them again.

Occasionally you'll even come across a twolegs with an actual, full-blown *phobia* about us. These ailurophobes undoubtedly won't stick around for long, but while they're there, why not amuse yourself? Hide until they relax, then throw all your energy reserves into a prodigious leap at their face, jaws wide, preferably screeching.

Curiosity, the fun and pitfalls of

Our nests, since they're built and decorated by humans, always have lots of unnecessary bric-a-brac around. Their entire lives are full of clutter, and they don't seem to need, use, or even know why they bought many of the items.

Nevertheless, it's all fun to examine, as long as certain dangers are borne in mind. By all means be curious; just be circumspect about your enquiries. Calamities often await on balconies and stoves, in plastic bags and washing machines, near light bulbs, candles, fireworks and the iron. Rubber bands, pills, antifreeze, cigarettes, toads and pieces of tinsel are not edible. Chimneys are usually best to leave alone, as are office shredding machines, rocking chairs, fans, plastic bags, wasps and bees, cacti and electric pruning shears. Don't get your flea collar caught on something that might drive away, don't chew those attractive electric wires, and remember that some plants have been ignorantly kept around even though they're poisonous, so don't nosh on those either.

And finally, we've found that the police kennels are definitely not worth investigating.

Tail, use and abuse of *(does not apply to Manx and Bobtail)*

Your tail is not only your anchor, your counterbalance, but a limb capable of its own expressive gestural language. A kind of postural punctuation. Needless to point out, *Homo sapiens* doesn't sport this articulate appendage, and misunderstands its signals on animals that do, so it may take some time to educate your servants in its semaphore.

The tail is capable of subtle meanings. For instance, if you suspect you're being ignored at breakfast you can easily whip your tail from human nostril to muesli and back again with no problem at all. As a statement of contempt, drag your tail across the face of a non-stroking biped or someone who smells of dog. As a casual remark of disdain, whack over an *objet d'art* — hopefully irreplaceable — or a vaseful of flowers. And as an expression of boredom, flick those car keys down the back of the sideboard where they won't be found for hours.

As always, watch out for locations or objects capable of amputation. And to the dangers listed under *Hiding* and *Curiosity* add electric fires, the waste disposal, the kitchen cutting board at salad time, and the toaster.

Conspiracy, theories of

Some non-cat admirers, probably those hostile *dog people*, think that cats are taking over.

It's true that there are upwards of seven million cats in the UK, and not nearly as many dogs. Our numbers have swollen to 56 million in the US, with that of dogs only at 51. In France, we're 7,500,000 strong, dogs a measly 6,000,000. This means that in modern industrial cities there are at least 1000 moggies per square mile. We're in every fourth house in Britain, and frankly we'd be in the rest if they weren't so awful.

But it's wrong to think of this as a conspiracy of speciewide proportions. This is not an attempt at takeover of the so-called human world by felines — this is a *fait accompli*. We succeeded some time ago, and are now reaping the rewards of our subtle, bloodless coup, our intimate invasion.

We are installed permanently in their flats, their semi-detacheds, their villas. We are ensconced forever in their garages, on their roofs, at their fireplaces. Darwin was right, and humans have been surpassed by the true evolutionary leader, the Cat, and live under our benign felinocracy.

And the best part is, they don't even know it.

Love, being the source of

Humans have a deep-seated need not only to *be* loved but to love back, and by far the greatest contribution catkind makes is the love we give them, and allow them to give us. They exchange it with each other too, but theirs is fragile and dependent on too many factors. Ours is unconditional.

Stroking us calms us both, so we're therapeutic. So much so, in fact, that we're employed in hospitals and nursing homes. The survival rate after a heart attack is higher in humans with a cat. Research even shows humans with cats live longer.

And why not? We give their lives meaning, focus. And we recharge their love batteries.

To be sure, we can be cranky and irritable, hard to please and a touch self-centred at times. But to a good human who treats us right we'll give — whenever we can — all our love.

It's a strange symbiosis we've forged over the years, but a positive one for all concerned. Two legs or four, big and bald or small and furry, we've learned to get along, and by doing so we represent a model of what life could be like for everyone.

Though of different persuasions, with different tastes and needs, we live together and it works.

also available in the same series:

MYSTERY OF CATS

KITTICULTURE

by David Westwood,
author of THE OFFICE MANUAL and THE LOVE MANUAL

TWO HEADS PUBLISHING
12A Franklyn Suite, The Priory
Haywards Heath, West Sussex RH16 3LB

ISBN 1 897850 90 5

Printed in Great Britain by Caldra House Ltd., Hove, Sussex
Bound by Butler & Tanner, Somerset

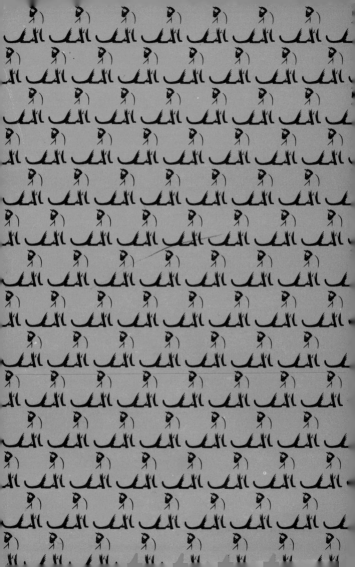